Cairns to Cooktown

David Heenan

GLENMEDE

Author and photographer,
David Heenan.

Published by Glenmede Pty Ltd
P.O. Box 291, Red Hill, Queensland,
Australia 4059
Telephone: 0417-618 493

First Published 1999
Copyright © David Heenan 1999

National Library of Australia Card Number ISBN 0 9577391 0 9

With Thanks

The author would like to thank the following organisations
and companies. Without their assistance the publication of
this book would not have been possible.

Contents

The Low Isles, east of Port Douglas. Quicksilver's beautiful "Wavedancer" catamaran, which sails here for day trips, is moored off-shore.

Introduction

Far North Queensland - particularly from Cairns to Cooktown - is an area of great beauty and diversity. It is where World Heritage listed rainforest meets another of Nature's marvels, the Great Barrier Reef.

Last century, the first Europeans were lured to the area by gold and valuable rainforest timbers. They were wild, pioneering days.

Today, the ancient rainforests are protected - and inhabited by a third of Australia's mammal species and a half of its bird species. The Great Barrier Reef harbours a multitude of colourful corals and over 1,500 species of fish.

Visitors cannot only enjoy these natural wonders but explore villages like Kuranda with its famous markets, enjoy some of the best game-fishing in the world, or escape to a beautiful island.

There is accommodation to suit all budgets from back-packer hostels and camp-sites to wilderness lodges and five-star hotels. In the evenings there are balmy, tropical nights and excellent restaurants to be discovered.

Few places in the world would offer as much to the visitor as the region between Cairns and Cooktown, and where the Rainforest meets the Reef. This book was designed to be a guide to all its best attractions - and to show its beauty, history, and local culture in a way never attempted before.

One of the many streams flowing through the Far North's dense rainforest.

This remarkable photographic image of the coastline between Cairns and Cooktown was captured by satellite.

The image covers approximately two hundred kilometres of North Queensland's coastline and was captured by a US satellite orbiting some 700 kilometres above the earth.

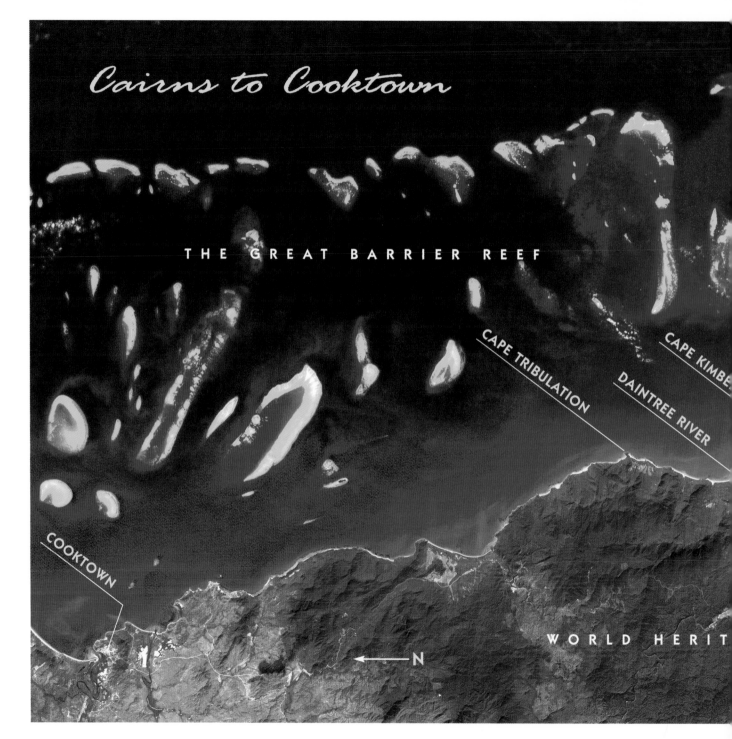

Cairns to Cooktown

THE GREAT BARRIER REEF

CAPE TRIBULATION

DAINTREE RIVER

CAPE KIMBE

COOKTOWN

WORLD HERIT

← N

CORAL SEA

CAIRNS

PALM COVE

KURANDA

PORT DOUGLAS

MAN

ATHERTON TABLELANDS

SYDNEY
2,140KMS

NFOREST

AUSTRALIA

CAIRNS

BRISBANE

SYDNEY
MELBOURNE

HOBART

The dense area of World Heritage Rainforest in the region is clearly visible, as are various islands and reefs off-shore which are part of Australia's spectacular Great Barrier Reef (which runs down the North Eastern coast of Australia for a distance of 2,500 kilometres).

LANDSAT imagery sourced from the Australian Centre for Remote Sensing (ACRES), AUSLIG (www.auslig.gov.au), provided through the Department of Natural Resources, Queensland.

7

A group of aborigines with Archibald Meston near the Daintree River, c. 1895. Meston studied and wrote on Aboriginal tribes and their customs.

A Colourful Past

Far North Queensland is rich in history. Europeans and many Chinese were among the very early settlers - drawn by the prospects of riches from goldfields and prized rainforest timbers like cedar which was known as "red gold". Other adventurers manned bêche-de-mer luggers, hoping to reap a fortune from the sea-bed of the Great Barrier Reef.

Long before any of these early pioneers arrived, however, the Cairns to Cooktown region was inhabited by aboriginal tribes who were a little different in physical appearance and life-style than aborigines living elsewhere in Australia. At least three tribes lived around the Trinity Inlet district where Cairns was established - the Irukandji, Idindji and Konkandji. Sea-foods were their staple diet and they used outrigger canoes to fish and travel along the coastline. Around Kuranda and to the north, there were rainforest dwelling tribes including the Djabgay, whilst on the Atherton Tablelands there was the Ngadyandyi tribe.

Sub-inspector Alexander Douglas, a man who actively promoted peace between the whites and blacks, reported in 1878 that there were at least 4,000 aborigines living between Cairns and the Daintree River.

Unfortunately, aborigines were ill-treated by some of the early European settlers and the natives no doubt resented the intrusion into their traditional living and hunting lands.

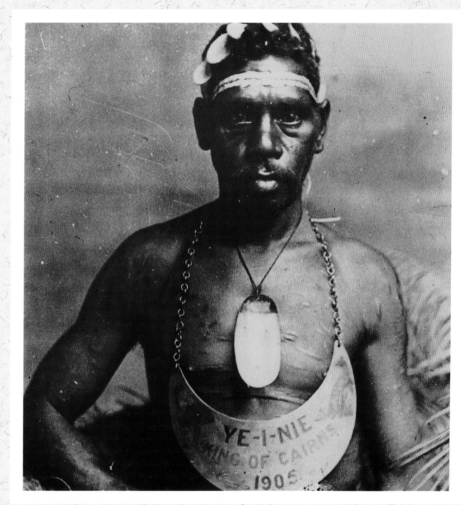

Ye-I-Nie, a tribal leader, photographed in 1905.

Aborigines in the Far North, unlike those elsewhere, used outrigger canoes.

Aborigines in the Cairns region, c. 1890's.

Miners and land seekers were subsequently attacked by hostile natives, who also ran off with cattle horses and cattle, and armed settlers fought back to protect their homes and families. Some Europeans wanted to help the natives and give them a fair deal but violent skirmishes, diseases previously unknown to them, and grog helped decimate the original population.

Today, however, ancestors of the original tribes still live in the region and there is a large aboriginal community of 2,500 people at Yarrabah (see page 28).

Trinity Bay, where Cairns is located, was named by Captain James Cook on his voyage of discovery up the Eastern coast of Australia in 1770 aboard the "Endeavour". The famous seaman almost came to grief after hitting a reef off Cape Tribulation, also named by him for obvious reasons. Fortunately, he eventually managed to repair his vessel at what is now named Cooktown.

Some of the other seaman who subsequently ventured into these northern waters after colonies were settled in the south were bêche-de-mer fishermen. Bêche-de-mer, or sea cucumbers, which live in the shallow waters of the Great Barrier Reef have been considered a delicacy in the East for hundreds of years. Once dried and smoked, it fetched between £80 and £140 a ton, a lucrative amount in the 1800's.

In the early 1800's the more populous regions in the south eagerly sought timber for construction. When explorer George Dalrymple reported the presence of vast stands of cedar between Cardwell and Cooktown, timbermen were quick to seize the opportunity. These tough, axe-wielding pioneers also laid the foundations of early settlements as farmers made use of the land cleared by logging - particularly on the Atherton Tablelands.

Settlement in Far North Queensland was hastened by the discovery of gold inland at the Palmer and Hodgkinson Rivers. Hordes of white and Chinese

The waterfront of Cairns as depicted in an early postcard.

The "Cairns Post" Newspaper was originally located in Lake Street.

The People's Cash Store, Cairns, 1914.

The early Cairns Railway Station.

Members of the Cairns Fire Brigade, c. 1920.

The Queensland National Bank, Cairns, was built in the 1880's.

prospectors flocked to the goldfields and Cooktown, Port Douglas and Cairns were established as ports to get vital supplies to the miners. Miners also came down to these places to get equipment, rest and have a good time.

All three ports were wild places where grog was consumed in vast quantities. It was initially sold from bush timber and bark shanty pubs and even carts in the main streets before hotels and other buildings were properly constructed. Houses of ill-repute flourished. The Chinese also established opium dens and illegal gambling houses - the Cairns Chinatown was in Sach's Street, now called Grafton Street.

The Chinese endured great animosity and racial abuse from the majority of early white miners and settlers. More Chinese prospectors were also ambushed by warring aborigines than whites. Some aborigines practised cannibalism and Chinese flesh was supposedly favoured by them because it was less salty than white men's! A more plausible reason is that more Chinese prospectors were killed simply because they were not as well armed.

Great numbers of Chinese returned to their homeland after the gold rushes but some remained to help forge the region's future. A syndicate of Chinese, who had saved money from the goldfields, established the first sugar cane plantation and mill just outside Cairns. Others became prominent merchants or established market gardens, and junks could often be seen transporting goods along inland waterways.

As more and more sugar cane plantations were established in the region, a severe shortage of labour resulted. At least two thousand native labourers were recruited from the Solomon and New Hebride Islands, and New Guinea. Many were well treated but unfortunately, some of the "Kanakas", as they were known, were actually kidnapped by unscrupulous seamen who scoured

A view of Port Douglas in 1914.

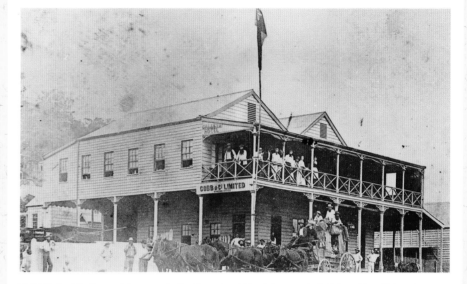

A Cobb & Co coach outside the Exchange Hotel, Port Douglas, c. 1884.

A cyclone devastated Port Douglas in 1911.

Four Mile Beach, Port Douglas, 1967.

Timber being hauled on the Atherton Tablelands, 1922.

A sawmill near Atherton, c. 1907.

Felling timber on the Atherton Tablelands in the 1890's.

the South Sea islands aboard schooners looking for hapless victims. These islanders were then sold as slave labour until Government legislation outlawed the despicable practice in 1885.

Stimulated by the gold-rushes, Cairns and Port Douglas became fierce commercial rivals and the latter was, at one stage, a busier port and trading centre than Cairns. It lost the upper hand, however, when Cairns won the bid in 1887 for a railway line that was to climb up the Barron Gorge to the Atherton Tablelands and serve the burgeoning settlements and mines beyond.

The building of this railway up such steep and treacherous terrain was an incredible engineering feat which stands as a lasting testimony to the ambitions, fortitude and suffering of hundreds of men engaged in its construction. The working conditions - in swamps and jungle - was almost unbearable. Bridges, tunnels and tracks were built using hand tools, dynamite, buckets and bare hands.

At least 23 deaths - and an untold number of accidents - were caused by tree felling, carelessness with explosives, falling rocks, men falling into the gorge, and drowning. Malaria, dysentery and snake-bite added to the workmen's woes. The railway, however, was completed and officially opened on 15th June, 1891 - and the future of the Tablelands, and Cairns, was assured.

From 1882 until the turn of the century, Australia's famous coach service, Cobb and Co., operated a service from Port Douglas. Coaches took a route over the Tablelands, through the silver-lead mining town of Montalbion and then onto Croydon, another mining town. In 1890 the company controlled 6,437 kilometres of passenger routes in Queensland alone but its demise was ultimately sealed as more rail tracks continued to open up.

There were many legendary characters in the Far North - even the late

The Hunter's Barron Falls Hotel, Kuranda.

The original Mossman to Daintree Road, c. 1933.

Cooktown's harbour in 1895.

Charlotte Street, Cooktown, c. 1874.

Hollywood star Errol Flynn played a minor role in the history of Cairns. When he was 24 and on his way to Port Moresby in 1931 aboard his yacht "Sirocco", Flynn was running short of money but still had enough to gamble with Italians and Chinese at the grand old Strand Hotel and Hotel Pacific (site now occupied by the Pacific International Hotel). Flynn was befriended by a dapper, well-educated Chinaman who offered him £60 to take his yacht out to Green Island to "collect a package". It was a package of opium. After collecting it, Flynn sailed on to Port Moresby, before making his screen debut in an Australian-made documentary called "In the Wake of the Bounty".

Green Island has a very interesting history, as does Fitzroy and Lizard Islands, the other two resort islands in the Cairns to Cooktown region.

Green Island was once used by aborigines for initiation ceremonies. In 1770 Captain Cook named it after his astronomer, Charles Green. It was later used as a base by bêche-de-mer fishermen, some of whom were attacked and killed by aborigines. In 1877, Fitzroy Island had 3,000 Chinese quarantined on it. Drawn to North Queensland by the lure of gold, they were confined on the island until they rioted over lack of food and shelter.

Captain Cook climbed to the top of Lizard Island in August, 1770, in the hope of finding a way out through the maze of reefs around it. In the 1870s it was the home of a bêche-de-mer fisherman Robert Watson and his wife Mary. Whilst he was away fishing, marauding aborigines arrived. Mary used a water tank as a make-shift boat to flee the island but subsequently perished from exposure and lack of water.

Although the wildest days of the Far North are now over, the region still has vast tracts of untamed wilderness - and some very colourful figures. Who knows, one may even discover more gold one day!

Charlotte Street, Cooktown, in 1888.

Mounted native police outside their Cooktown barracks, c. 1878.

A Cooktown shop-front and townspeople in 1897.

Tropical Cairns

The cruise-ship "Fairstar" approaching Marlin Marina and Trinity Wharf, Cairns.

Cairns, the unofficial capital of Far North Queensland, was originally established at Trinity Inlet in October, 1876. It was named after Sir William Wellington Cairns, the Irish-born Governor of Queensland of that era.

Cairns, like Port Douglas, was established as a port following the discovery of the Hodgkinson goldfields, although Trinity Inlet had previously been used by bêche-de-mer fishermen seeking their fortunes in the waters of the Coral Sea.

After the gold rush, Cairns prospered because of its large sugar cane plantations (the first was actually established by a syndicate of Chinese who were originally lured to the area by the riches of the goldfields).

Today, Cairns is a city of 100,000 people that draws thousands more each year from all around the world, attracted by the beauty of the surrounding rainforest, islands, reefs, and rugged mountains - as well as leisure pursuits like fishing, golfing, and white water rafting.

Cairns has its own International Airport, a casino, hotels of world-class standard, dozens of motels, apartments and hostel accommodation for backpackers.

It is a small relaxed city with tree-lined streets, pavement cafes, old pubs, restaurants, arcades, boutiques, and duty free shops where you can buy everything from local souvenirs to superb jewellery, and fashions by top Australian and overseas designers.

Serious shoppers will find much to tempt them at The Pier Marketplace, a place where a market is also held on Saturdays, Sundays and public holidays. Stalls offer a wide variety of well-made local arts and crafts, jewellery, and fashion. Another outdoor market is open each night between 5pm and 11pm, mid-way along The Esplanade.

Yachts and game-fishing boats are berthed at Marlin Marina.

The distinctive colonial-style architecture of Cairns' city centre.

The Bolands Centre, on the corner of Spence and Lake Streets.

The Cairns Post building is classified by the National Trust.

The city centre has a casual, tropical mood.

Cairns has a number of small art galleries with exceptional work available by talented local artists, reflecting the many subjects and differing moods of the Tropics. Some well-known Aboriginal artists are represented, too. Art lovers should also pay a visit to the Cairns Regional Art Gallery (open daily), at the corner of Abbott and Shields Streets.

Those interested in the colourful history of Cairns should visit the small but excellent Museum (open daily), run by the Cairns Historical Society. Located on the first floor of the old School of Arts building at the corner of Shields and Lake Streets, it houses many fascinating historical items and old photographs that portray the life of past generations. Included is a collection of Aboriginal artifacts once belonging to the rainforest dwellers of the Cairns district, the contents of a former Cairns Chinese Joss House, and relics from the Palmer River and Hodgkinson Goldfields.

Many examples of early architecture.

A legacy of earlier generations can also be found in the distinctive architecture of the old public buildings and high-standing timber houses in and around Cairns. The homes are known as "Queenslanders", and they stand high off the ground on wooden "stilts" to help keep the interiors cool. They can also be easily recognised by their corrugated iron roofs and wide verandahs which offer wonderful protection both from the sun and from tropical downpours of rain.

An excellent restored example of one of these classic homes is Cominos House on the corner of Greenslope and Little Streets, Edge Hill. It houses an Art and Environment Centre, and is open to the public.

Opposite Cominos House are the Centenary Lakes. A large variety of birds can be seen here, and a boardwalk through a wetland connects this area

Cominos House, a beautifully restored building in Edge Hill.

One of the many classic high-built "Queenslanders" in Cairns.

The Pier Marketplace, the Radisson Plaza Hotel and Marlin Marina at night-time.

The Pier also has an indoor market on weekends.

with the Flecker Botanic Gardens in Collins Avenue. These beautiful gardens feature a Fernery, Orchid House, Aboriginal plant use section, as well as palms, tropical fruits and flowering trees, shrubs and vines. Admission is free. The Botanic Gardens, which are approximately four kilometres from the City Centre, are open every day until 5:30 pm.

Adjacent to the Botanic Gardens is the entrance to Mt. Whitfield Environmental Park which has two walking tracks and several look-outs that provide sweeping views of Cairns and Trinity Inlet. The large majestic Cassowary, large flightless birds, can sometimes be seen in the Park as well as Brush Turkeys, Scrub Hens and Wallabies. Along the way you may notice the

A view encompassing the Reef Hotel Casino, the Hilton Hotel and Trinity Inlet.

fruits of the Blue Quandong and the Kuranda Quandong - these berries are the favoured fruits of Cassowaries and brilliantly hued Fruit Doves.

One walking track is 1.3 kilometres long and takes an easy hour to complete. Along it are 81 identified native plants. The second circuit is a rugged bush track 5.4 kilometres long. This track has some steep climbs and takes four to five hours to complete but has some wonderful views.

Also in Edge Hill, and open daily, is the Royal Flying Doctor Visitors Centre. The Flying Doctors have provided a medical service to outback communities and homesteads since 1912, and this centre explains how this famous service operates, and has many exhibits and memorabilia on display.

A large cruise ship docks at Trinity Wharf.

The beautiful Paradise Palms Resort golf course with Double Island and the Coral Sea visible in the background.

At Marlin Jetty, at the mouth of Trinity Inlet, you can take cruises out to the Reef and beautiful islands like Michaelmas Cay, Upolu Cay, Green Island and Fitzroy Island (details about these destinations can be found on page 78 of this book). You can also explore the mangrove fringed waterways of Trinity Inlet, home to many salt water crocodiles - or cruise to Redbank Crocodile Farm, operated by the Pormpuraaw Aboriginal Community, where there are 3,000 crocodiles and crocodile hatchlings in captivity.

Those interested in Nature can also walk along a long boardwalk through mangrove forest, just off Airport Avenue. The boardwalk weaves through a forest of 11 different mangrove species. Mangroves are a valuable nursery ground for sea creatures and more than 60 per cent of the commercial fish-eries catch comprises species dependent on mangrove areas.

Many thrills awaiting game-fishermen.

The waters off Cairns are a fisherman's paradise. They offer some of the best game-fishing in the world, with Black Marlin weighing up to 1,600 lbs (725 kilograms) regularly being caught. Fortunately, most of these mighty fish are now tagged and then released. The game-fishing season for Black Marlin is between September and December but light-tackle fishing is a popular pas-time all year round. Spanish Mackerel, Tuna, and Trevally are just some of the fish commonly caught. The game-fishing fleet is based at Marlin Marina, alongside the Pier Marketplace. The Cairns Game Fishing Club is a stone's throw away, and visitors are welcome.

Reef fishing charters also leave daily from the Marlin Jetty - and it's a rare day when there is not a good catch of delicious fish like Coral Trout, Red Emperor and Sweetlip. Fishing trips up the river estuaries are available, too - fish caught include Mangrove Jack, King Salmon, Barramundi and Queenfish.

Greg Norman plays in a championship game at Paradise Palms.

This massive Black Marlin, that eluded capture, was thought to weigh about 1,500 lbs.

Palm Cove, one of the Northern Beaches of Cairns, and home to several secluded resorts.

Exploring The Marlin Coast.

Heading out of Cairns to the north, on the Captain Cook Highway, you will find the Northern Beaches. This area is known, too, as the Marlin Coast and a string of beaches and small coves stretch up the coastline for 26 kilometres - Machans Beach, Holloways Beach, Yorkeys Knob, Trinity Beach, Kewarra Beach, Clifton Beach, Palm Cove and Ellis Beach.

Probably the most popular of these beaches for visitors to the region is secluded Palm Cove. It has a village atmosphere, several excellent hotels, holiday apartments and beachside restaurants.

Nearby, golfers can enjoy a challenging championship course at Paradise Palms Golf Course. Designed by Australian championship golfer Graham Marsh, this beautifully maintained resort course has hosted some of the world's most prestigious golf tournaments. (Cairns Golf Club, surrounded partially by magnificent mountains, has another course recommended by many. There is also a golf course at Yorkeys Knob and a nine-hole course at the Novotel Palm Cove Resort.)

It should be apparent by now that Cairns is a very convenient and enjoyable base for an almost endless list of different day-time activities and excursions. At night-time, there is a wide choice of restaurants to please all taste-buds - seafood, Mediterranean, Asian, and others specialising in Australian Cuisine (offering menus with emu, crocodile, kangaroo dishes prepared with delicious wild fruits and vegetables, known and enjoyed only by aborigines until more recent times).

The original founders of Cairns would not recognise the city today. Relaxed and cosmopolitan, and basking in a tropical climate, Cairns seems destined to become even better known as one of Australia's premier destinations.

A more unusual way to explore the beach at Palm Cove.

Palm Cove has an unrushed, village atmosphere.

Children living at Yarrabah down at the sea-front at Mission Bay.

The Local Aborigines

Various aboriginal tribes lived in the Cairns to Cooktown region long before the arrival of European settlers - and today aborigines still live throughout the whole area. Many traditions and customs are still maintained by the indigenous people and different tribes still have their own dialects.

In earlier generations there were many customs and rites no longer practised. When the king of a tribe went in search of a wife, for example, he made a cut on the girl's shoulder so that she would never forget him. To be king he had to possess two cuts on each shoulder. Every boy who reached the age of twelve received a cut by the chief or oldest man of the tribe. Other cuts followed and it was not unusual for a fully grown man to have as many as a dozen cuts.

Today, visitors to the region have the opportunity to experience something of the traditional aboriginal culture (details page 32) - and beautiful, locally hand-made aboriginal artifacts are also available in some shops and stalls at local markets like Kuranda's.

The Aboriginal Community of Yarrabah.

The largest single group of aborigines live at Yarrabah, an aboriginal community east of Cairns. The community's land, owned by the Yarrabah Aboriginal Council, covers a 154 kilometre square coastal strip which encompasses the Grafton Peninsula. Most of its inhabitants reside in a township overlooking Mission Bay.

Aboriginal artifacts made at Yarrabah.

Two fishermen roll up their net after a fishing expedition.

Yarrabah was originally established in the 1890's by the Rev. John Gribble who was concerned about the welfare and protection of the indigenous people at a time when more white settlers had arrived – and fierce fighting between the two parties had resulted in many casualties. Sadly, many aborigines were also maltreated.

Some of the houses at Yarrabah in the early 1900's.

Today, Yarrabah is home to some 2,500 aborigines. The community is now governed by an aboriginal council and is self-sufficient in many ways. The community has its own primary and high schools, hospital, shops, and bakery.

Whilst access to Yarrabah is reserved for the aborigines who live there, all are welcome to visit the Museum which has a very interesting and extensive display of old aboriginal artifacts and photographs which documents the community's history.

The Museum is generally open between 8:00am and 4:30pm, Mondays to Fridays, but it is worth phoning 07-4056 9154 in advance of your intended visit to ensure that it will be open.

Les Murgha, Chairperson of the Gungandji tribe (top right), and children attending Yarrabah's own school.

Experience Aboriginal Culture.

One experience that should not be missed by those visiting the region is the Tjapukai Aboriginal Cultural Park, Smithfield, on the outskirts of Cairns.

The Park is a partnership involving the local Tjapukai, Yirrgandyji and Djabugay tribes.

The Park sets out to preserve and present the ancient aboriginal culture. There are five theatres, a museum, an art gallery and traditional Aboriginal camp.

In the museum there are stone age artifacts once used by the Tjapukai tribe and large murals by aboriginal artists depict legends of the past. In the Creation Theatre the spiritual and traditional beliefs of the Tjapukai people are portrayed, with performers interacting with animated images. The History Theatre shows and tells the history of the last 120 years of how aborigines met the modern world.

The award-winning Tjapukai Dance Theatre gives you the opportunity of viewing segments of traditional corroborees, a celebration of song and dance. The Traditional Camp gives you the chance to mix with members of the aboriginal community, learn about bush foods and medicines, and to try your hand at boomerang and spear throwing, and didgeridoo playing.

The Tjapukai Aboriginal Cultural Park is open between 9am and 5pm daily (except Christmas day and New Year's Day), and shows run continuously throughout the day.

Five minutes from Kuranda, on the Kennedy Highway, you can also visit Rainforestation, set in 40 hectares of World Heritage rainforest. Here Pamagirri Aboriginal dancers perform daily and you can also try your hand at spear and boomerang throwing.

Locally made aboriginal artifacts on sale at the Kuranda Markets.

Dancers who perform at the acclaimed Tjapukai Aboriginal Cultural Park.

The Atherton Tablelands

The cleared, rolling hills of the Atherton Tableland have been used for dairy farming since last century.

Behind Cairns the landscape is dominated by a spectacular mountain range, often shrouded in cloud or mist. Atop this range is the Atherton Tablelands, an area of stunning beauty and diversity.

Up until 100,000 years ago the Tablelands were subject to great volcanic activity, and today the area's turbulent geological history is reflected in its rugged mountains, volcanic crater lakes, spectacular waterfalls, beautiful streams and rivers, rolling hills and rich farming soil.

The Tablelands - which are between 600 and 1,000 metres above sea level - also have some of the world's oldest and most luxuriant rainforest, preserved in National Parks. Giant Kauri trees, large primitive ferns, a myriad of tree dwelling plants, mosses and lichens can all be viewed here as they could have been seen thousands of years ago.

It was the lure of Kauri and Red Cedar - sometimes referred to as 'red gold' - that first drew people to the Tablelands. Felling these mighty trees was one challenge - an even greater one was getting it to civilisation. Teams of 20 bullocks were often used until rail lines were built.

Clearing of forests led to dairying and agriculture. The first settlers were true pioneers, enduring many hardships - and there are a number of charming villages and old pubs on The Tablelands dating back to those early days. In short, a visit to The Tablelands should not be missed.

Travellers can basically travel in a circular loop from Cairns, taking the Bruce Highway south, heading in-land on the Palmerston Highway and travelling back up through Malanda and Yungaburra, or through the township of Atherton and Kuranda. Whilst this can be achieved in one day, you could easily spend several days exploring the Tablelands.

To the southern end of the Tablelands - about one hour from Cairns - is

The famous Curtain Fig Tree at Yungaburra National Park.

A sculpture of an early timber-getter outside the historic Peeramon Pub.

Bellenden Ker National Park. Queensland's highest peak, Mt. Bartle Frere (1,622 metres high), and Josephine Falls can be found here. White water rafting and canoeing can be enjoyed on the North Johnstone River. There are many walking tracks through the lush, tropical rainforest. Wildlife include golden bower birds, tree-climbing kangaroos, and up to 100 species of birds.

West of Bellenden Ker National Park are the famous Millaa Millaa Falls. North-west of here is Mount Hypipamee National Park - centred around an ancient water-filled crater 70 metres across.

Further north is the historic village of Yungaburra which has many turn-of-the-century buildings, still in near perfect condition. The small Yungaburra National Park features a gigantic Curtain Fig Tree and nearby are two beautiful crater lakes, Lake Eacham and Lake Barrine, surrounded by massive rainforest trees up to 55 metres high.

The giant kauri pines that can be seen here and elsewhere on The Tableland are almost identical to fossil kauris found in rocks around 300 million years old.

Another well-known attraction just 100 metres off the Danbulla Forest Drive - a 28 kilometre unsealed road running from the Gillies Highway to Tolga, just north of Atherton - is the legendary 500 year-old Cathedral Fig. It is as high as a twelve storey building and has a girth of 43 metres. The Cathredal Fig has a cavernous interior and an abundance of bird-life and small animals call the tree home. Lumholtz's Tree Kangaroo, Green-tailed possums, Long-nosed Bandicoots and Musky Rat-Kangaroos are some of the animals seen in or around it.

The Tablelands is a truly historic area, abounding with natural scenic beauty and wildlife. No visit to the Cairns region would be complete without sampling at least some of its many attractions.

A restaurant in the quaint old village of Yungaburra.

An old building alongside the Yungaburra sawmill.

The Cuckoo Clock Gallery on the outskirts of Yungaburra.

Peeramon Pub, the oldest hotel on the Tablelands.

The peaceful Mulgrave River, alongside the Gillies Highway which climbs up to the Tablelands.

Picturesque Millaa Millaa Falls, just over 20 kilometres south of Malanda.

The misty view from Crawford Lookout, overlooking the North Johnstone River.

White water rafting on the North Johnstone River.

The scenic Kuranda Train climbs 328 metres from Cairns and passes many spectacular sights.

Kuranda

Few people visiting North Queensland would want to miss a visit to Kuranda, often described as "The Village in the Rainforest". There is much to see and do here - and visitors should allow at least one full day to enjoy the journey to Kuranda, its famous markets, and other attractions.

Kuranda is just 27 kilometres north-west of Cairns. Unlike Cairns, however, which sits on the low coastal strip adjoining the Coral Sea, Kuranda lies near the edge of the McAlister mountain range which rises up sharply just a few kilometres inland to form the Atherton Tablelands.

The small township, which was officially established in 1888, is located alongside the tranquil Barron River which plunges suddenly and dramatically downstream at the nearby Barron Falls.

In its early days, Kuranda was settled primarily by people working on the railway which helped open up the vast Atherton Tablelands for saw-milling operations and farmers. The first crop grown in the immediate vicinity of Kuranda was coffee beans and Alf Street, one of the first growers, won prizes in London and Paris for his high quality coffee.

Kuranda and the nearby Falls started to attract tourists at the turn of the century and the village and its hotels were particularly popular with honeymooners. In the late 1960's hippies discovered Kuranda. In the 1970's people espousing alternative life-styles built simple, unusual homes of local brick and timber. Their colourful influence has remained.

Many of the locals lead unorthodox life-styles.

The thundering Barron Falls in full flow during the Wet Season.

Today, visitors from all over the globe seem to be irresistibly drawn to this small village. There are now three ways to get to Kuranda - by road, train or Skyrail Rainforest Cableway. If time limits you to spending just one day at Kuranda, the author suggests you travel one way by train, the other by Skyrail.

The scenic journey by train, along an historic railway track completed in 1891, takes about one and a half hours. The train winds its way up and around almost one hundred curves on its way to Kuranda, goes through 15 tunnels and passes by waterfalls that will take your breath away before finally arriving at one of the world's most picturesque railway stations.

Travelling by Skyrail Rainforest Cableway, which opened in 1995, is also an unforgettable experience. Running for seven and a half kilometres from Smithfield, just north of Cairns, this aerial cableway gives all passengers - suspended in gondolas high above the ground - a stunning bird's-eye view of dense rainforest canopy and panoramic views over the entire district.

If you are travelling up to Kuranda by Skyrail you will first enjoy spectacular views back to Cairns and out towards the Great Barrier Reef. On a clear day both Green and Fitzroy Islands are visible. Just before you reach Kuranda on Skyrail you will look back down the deep and rugged Barron Gorge.

Along the way there are two Skyrail stations. The first is Red Peak, 545 metres above sea level. At Red Peak there is a board-walk which takes you through rainforest where you can observe vegetation at close hand. The second Skyrail station is at Barron Falls where there is also a Rainforest Information Centre. As the name suggests, this station affords a view of the Barron Falls from a small lookout framed by rainforest.

A more famous lookout with even more expansive views of the Falls is the one on the opposite side of the Gorge. The Barron Falls Lookout has been a

Looking up the steep Barron Gorge towards Kuranda.

The Board-walk at Red Peak.

Skyrail's cableway travels more than seven kilometres over ancient rainforest.

Skyrail gives a bird's eye view of the rainforest.

A local character outside the Kuranda Hotel, built in 1882.

popular scenic destination for over 100 years, and in the Wet Season the sight of the Falls from this vantage point is awesome, and the noise thunderous, as the flood of water plummets almost 300 metres. This lookout is situated about three kilometres from Kuranda, along Barron Falls Road.

A bustling Village on Market Days.

Kuranda is a relaxed village of shady trees, old timber houses, pubs, shops, galleries and small, casual eating places. The village is alive with activity on market days - held on Wednesdays, Thursdays, Fridays and Sundays. On market days dozens of colourful stalls offer a wide array of items - mostly handmade - including didgeridoos, wood carvings, pottery, jewellery, leather bags, clothing and paintings.

Towards the northern end of the village are another two attractions - the Australian Butterfly Sanctuary and the Wildlife Noctarium.

The Butterfly Sanctuary is the largest butterfly farm in the country. The enclosed aviary is home to up to 2,500 tropical butterflies of 14 different species. The Wildlife Noctarium, a stone's throw away, allows you to experience the rainforest as it is at night-time - and see many interesting creatures that are only visible and active at night.

Just five minutes from Kuranda, on the Kennedy Highway, you can also visit Rainforestation, set in 40 hectares of World Heritage rainforest. Here Pamagirri Aboriginal dancers perform daily and you can also try your hand at spear and boomerang throwing.

An early brochure, written in the 1930's, encouraged readers to "come to Kuranda for a tonic, for a rest, to enjoy the best mountain air, the most golden sunshine and the richest sight of tropical jungle." This and much, much more awaits the visitor today.

A sample of the scores of stalls at the Kuranda Market.

Captain Cook Highway

An aerial view of beautiful Wangetti Beach.

One of the most scenic drives in Australia is unquestionably the one between Cairns and Port Douglas. Hugging the Marlin Coast for most of the way to Port Douglas, this road is known as the Captain Cook Highway.

The distance between Cairns and Port Douglas is only 67 kilometres but travellers should plan a very leisurely trip to take in all the marvellous unspoiled sights along this gently winding road. They will be treated to a string of beautiful, near-deserted coral beaches, pretty coves, majestic mountains, archways of trees and countless ferns dotting the landscape alongside the road.

About half way to Port Douglas there is another attraction – the Hartleys Creek Crocodile Farm. People can safely view monstrous specimens of these fearsome creatures here – and see them hand fed by their intrepid keepers. There is also a Snake Show in the early afternoon – and the opportunity to see both koalas and kangaroos.

North of the Hartleys Creek Crocodile Farm the Captain Cook Highway climbs up to Rex's Lookout, where the traveller can enjoy magnificent views of beautiful Wangetti Beach far below and the azure colours of the Coral Sea. Colourful hang-gliders can often be seen hovering high over Wangetti Beach.

Close to Port Douglas the Highway turns inland and continues for another 14 kilometres to the small township of Mossman, passing through very green sugar growing country. Here the highway officially ends but a continuation of this road then leads into the wilderness area of Cape Tribulation.

The coastline between Cairns and Port Douglas is unspoiled and uncrowded.

A view of the spectacular coastline stretching from Turtle Cove to Port Douglas.

Looking south along Wangetti Beach from Rex's Lookout.

The Marina at Port Douglas is the departure point for Reef cruises, diving and fishing charters.

Port Douglas

Port Douglas was officially established as a port in June, 1877. It was first known as Terrigal, Island Point, Port Owen and Salisbury but was finally named after the Queensland Premier of the late 1870's, John Douglas.

Many would argue that it was really put on the map by Christie Palmerston, a colourful adventurer and trailblazer, who found a track that would allow wagons to travel down to the coast from the newly discovered Hodgkinson goldfields. Palmerston found and named the Mowbray River - at the southern end of palm fringed Four Mile Beach - and news of the sheltered anchorage just a little to the north soon brought boats carrying diggers and settlers. A bustling township quickly began to take shape.

The port was so busy in those early days, that it seemed destined to replace Cairns as the unofficial capital of North Queensland. By 1879 Port Douglas had more than 20 hotels, and its population grew to 8,000.

Port Douglas eventually lost the race to its rival, however, when sugar cane growers were attracted to the Cairns district and Cairns won a hard-fought political campaign to become the major coastal link for the new railway line that was to run across the Atherton Tableland. By the mid-1900's the population of Port Douglas had fallen to around 100 inhabitants. Matters were not helped when a cyclone flattened much of the town in 1911.

During the 1960's and 1970's, however, it became "a best kept secret" amongst an increasing number of tourists drawn to the sun-drenched Tropics.

The Shipwreck Museum which houses relics from historic wrecks.

Fishermen return to port after a night's work.

The fleet of fishing trawlers at Port Douglas.

By the 1980's the sleepy little port had blossomed into a highly desirable tourist destination - and it's "laid-back" village atmosphere has been attracting visitors from Australia and many parts of the world ever since. Many rich and famous people have escaped temporarily to Port Douglas including Mick Jagger, Jerry Hall and Tom Cruise but perhaps its most famous visitor was U.S. President Bill Clinton who holidayed here in November, 1996.

Most have stayed at the luxurious Sheraton-Mirage Resort which sits alongside Four Mile Beach and which boasts an 18-hole championship golf course designed by five times British Open Champion Peter Thompson. There is accommodation at Port Douglas, however, to suit all pockets - including apartments, motels, hostels, and caravan parks.

The Daintree River is just 50 kilometres north of Port Douglas, so access to the ancient lowland rainforest in the Cape Tribulation National Park is easy. Pretty Mossman Gorge, territory of the Kuku Yalanji aborigines, is even closer.

You can find a sample of what these National Parks hold at the award-winning Rainforest Habitat just on the outskirts of Port Douglas, just off the Captain Cook Highway. Here you can see 65 species of birds and butterflies, koalas, crocodiles and kangaroos in an eco-system closely matching the natural environment.

From Port Douglas there are also some excellent day trips to the Outer Reef, where you can snorkel, dive or view colourful marine life in semi-submersible craft. Another popular day-trip is the one to the Low Isles, small and beautiful coral cays.

Vessels leave from Marina Mirage, an attraction in its own right. Scores of beautiful yachts and power boats bob gently at their berths, some available for day charter, reef fishing and game-fishing. There is also a beautiful shopping

An aerial photograph of Port Douglas, looking south towards Cairns.

A view of Sheraton Mirage, resort to the rich and famous.

arcade at the marina, and several restaurants.

A delightful paddlewheeler, appropriately named the "Lady Douglas", also departs from the marina four times daily and cruises the waterways of Port Douglas. With "Eco Cruises" you can also explore the local mangrove forests, learn about their importance, and see many of the 70 species of birds which inhabit the area. This small cruise company is a member of the Bird Observers Club of Australia - and supplies both binoculars and bird identification lists for keen bird-watchers.

Down at the waterfront you will also find The Shipwreck Museum, established by adventurer Ben Cropp, where you will see relics from the "Endeavour", and the "Pandora" (wrecked in 1791 on a reef en route from Tahiti after capturing mutineers from the "Bounty").

On Sundays a market is held in Anzac Park adjacent to the Museum. Colourful stalls offer fresh fruit, beautiful orchids, garments, baskets and other handcrafts made by modern-day hippies living in nearby rainforest hideaways. The handcrafts are usually of high quality.

People staying in Port Douglas also have the opportunity of enjoying a day excursion to Weatherby Station, forty five minutes inland, on the edge of Cape York's cattle country. Here you can see what life is really like on a Queensland cattle station, see stockmen give an exhibition of expert horsemanship, and enjoy a hearty "bushman's lunch".

Being the closest port to the Great Barrier Reef, and lying at the doorstep of ancient World Heritage Rainforest, Port Douglas has two unbeatable natural attractions. Combined with notable restaurants, and accommodation to suit all budgets, secluded Port Douglas can only continue to attract visitors from all over the world.

The Central Hotel, in Macrossan Street, was established in 1886.

Palms and trees line the streets of the small town centre.

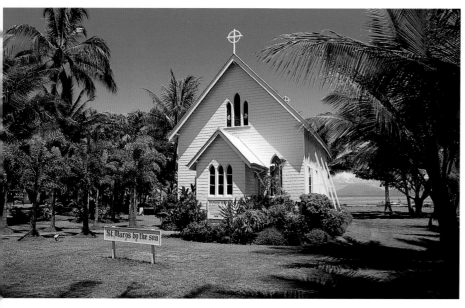

St. Mary's Church by the Sea dates back to 1880.

The Court House Hotel, in Wharf Street, was built in 1878.

The tranquil view from the tip of the Port Douglas headland looking north.

A yachting regatta takes place off Four Mile Beach.

Over 150 species of plants have been identified in the dense rainforest around Mossman Gorge.

Mossman River

Mossman River Gorge is 19 kilometres from Port Douglas, 86 kilometres from Cairns, and just five kilometres from the small township of Mossman.

Mossman Gorge is the only easily accessible section of the Daintree National Park, a rugged, uninhabited, mountainous area that covers 56,500 hectares - and most of it is covered by lush, dense rainforest.

The park is an area of high rainfall and the high volume of water feeding into the Mossman River has enabled it to carve out a steep sided valley where crystal-clear water tumbles over huge granite boulders. There are also a number of tranquil rock-pools which are ideal for swimming in.

Brilliant blue Ulysses butterflies and large green and black Cairns Birdwing butterflies can often be seen flitting over the river. In the river itself, jungle perch can be easily spotted and in the calmer parts of the river you may see a freshwater turtle or possibly even a platypus surfacing to breathe.

Bird-watchers can sight a variety of birds including beautiful blue Buff-breasted Paradise Kingfishers, Grey-headed Robins, and White-rumped Swiflets.

A circuit walk of just under three kilometres gives you the opportunity to view many rainforest trees, shrubs, vines, ferns, mosses and lichens. Over 150 different species have now been discovered in the local area and you will find that some have been labelled by the Queensland Parks and Wildlife Service for easy identification.

A side-stream running into Mossman River.

Canoeists from Silky Oaks Lodge explore a section of the Mossman River.

The Mossman River upstream from the Silky Oaks Wilderness Lodge.

Daintree to Cape Tribulation

Noah's Creek is about 20 kilometres drive north of the Daintree River and 10 kilometres south of Cape Tribulation.

The famous Daintree River lies just over one hundred kilometres north of Cairns. The river marks the southern border of Cape Tribulation National Park, which stretches north to the Bloomfield River and west to the rugged McDowall Range.

This is a very important and significant part of North Queensland's Wet Tropics region, which is a living museum of animals and plants that trace their ancestry back more than 100 million years. The region was listed for preservation as a World Heritage site in 1988.

The diversity of fauna and flora within the Wet Tropics is quite astonishing. It contains a third of Australia's mammal species; a half of its bird species; almost a quarter of its frogs; and a quarter of its reptiles. Many of the species are found only within this region.

The Daintree area is perhaps the most famous section of the Wet Tropics region, attracting well-known naturalists such as Dr. Susuki, Dr. Walter Starck and Sir David Attenborough. It is the only area where rainforest extends down to the coast and fringing coral reefs.

During the 1980's there was much controversy surrounding the logging activities and building of roads north of the Daintree. The media attention it generated has helped to make the area even more popular as a destination.

Most but not all of the land between the Daintree and Bloomfield rivers is National Park. There are private land holdings and some small settlements.

There are also a number of wilderness lodges north of the Daintree and visitors wishing to explore the area should consider camping or staying overnight in one of these lodges. Day-trips are offered from Cairns by various operators but these trips can be a little rushed because of the time needed to reach the area, and to return before evening sets in.

A giant fern frames a distant view of Cape Tribulation.

The Large Egret is one of many birds seen along the Daintree.

A Crocodile basks on the bank of the Daintree.

Once upon a time the road to Cape Tribulation was considered suitable only for 4-wheel drive vehicles but most of it is now sealed, so conventional vehicles can make the trip with relative ease.

The Daintree River is crossed by ferry which operates between 6:00 am and midnight all year round except on Christmas day and Easter Sunday.

On the southern side of the river, before the ferry crossing, is a wharf where you can join a river cruise - and these guided tours are highly recommended. There is a good chance that you will see a salt-water crocodile basking on the river-bank, and as you venture up smaller estuaries crowded by mangroves you are likely to catch sight of many species of birds. In fact, it is not uncommon to spot up to 50 different species on such a cruise.

The Daintree River actually originates in the Great Dividing Range near Mossman, and is about 135 kilometres in length. Smaller rivers run into it, along with thousands of streams.

The last 22 kilometres of the Daintree is a tidal estuary where warm salt water from the Coral Sea meets cold fresh water from up-river. Within these 22 kilometres some 200 species of fish can be found.

The banks of the river in the tidal area are fringed by mangroves, plants whose tube-like roots are exposed as the tide drops. Mangroves have often been dismissed in the past as being of little worth but nothing could be further from the truth. They form part of an important food chain - their leaves, when they fall into the water, break down into important nutrients which marine life are dependant on. Mangroves provide perfect breeding grounds for many fish, including Australia's famed Barramundi.

As mangroves flower they also attract nectar-eating birds, bats and insects. These then attract insect-eating birds. As fruit is formed, fruit-eaters and

An aerial view of the Daintree River. A ferry is crossing to its northern bank.

The large flightless Cassowary feeds on rainforest fruit.

Twenty three different species of frogs inhabit the rainforest.

seed-eaters are provided with food.

The crocodiles, incidentally, that can often be seen sun-baking on the banks of the Daintree River can grow up to 20 feet or almost seven metres in length. These awesome predators come from a very ancient group of creature - their ancestors were actually around before the great age of dinosaurs.

Once you have crossed the Daintree by ferry, the road winds up the rang and after about 15 minutes you will reach Alexandra Lookout, which afford spectacular views over the river and towards Cape Tribulation.

As you continue north you cannot help but notice Thornton Peak. Thi mountain is 1,375 metres high and is usually enveloped by cloud. It receive up to 6,000 mm of rainfall each year - almost twice that received on the coas - and is covered by thick vine-fern forest that few have penetrated.

Twenty eight kilometres from the ferry, at Oliver Creek, is the Marrdj Botanical Boardwalk which will take you 800 metres through rainforest to mangrove forest. There are interpretive signs along the way and many of th plants and trees are labelled.

Whether you choose to explore the cool, damp rainforest along this board walk or along any other other track, you will pass the buttressed trunks o massive trees that reach up high to the sky. Their upper branches form canopy that virtually blocks out the sun. Giant vines spiral up the tree trunks At ground level there are mosses and fungi, and a thick blanket of decompos ing leaves. As you brush past ferns and palms - and hear a primeval sound trac of clicks and screeches - it's easy to accept that life here has changed little i eons of time.

Whilst the colour green is almost synonymous with rainforest, some plant also produce brightly coloured fruits and flowers, including some 150 differen

The area north of the Daintree is a wilderness area of great beauty - and natural hazards.

The rainforest of Far North Queensland was listed as a World Heritage site in 1988.

species of orchards. Many visitors may not know that the rainforest also ha many species of native gingers.

One plant to avoid is the Stinging Shrub, often found in sunny areas along-side walking tracks. Its broad leaves and and stems are covered by tiny hairs o silica (the main component of glass) which easily penetrate the skin. When touched, the plant also releases a poison that can irritate the skin for months.

About 70 mammals inhabit the rainforest but as many of these are noctur-nal you are unlikely to see them during daylight but you may well see geckos the Boyd's Forest Dragon (a large lizard that grows up to 45 cm in length) small beautiful tree frogs, and colourful butterflies like the Cairns Birdwin (which has a wingspan up to 25 centimetres), and the iridescent blue Ulysses

You might also be fortunate enough to see an unusual species of kangaroo - the Tree Kangaroo. Unlike their more common counterparts who live on the ground, Lumholtz's Tree Kangaroos have powerful, heavily-clawed foreleg for gripping branches, and their hind-legs are shorter. They live on leaves and fruits in the rainforest.

Remember that most activity in the rainforest - apart from night-time - i at dawn or dusk, another reason to camp or a stay in a lodge where access i easy. Some wilderness lodges also offer night-time guided tours of the rain-forest with spotlights.

Another path and elevated boardwalk at Cape Tribulation also takes you through rainforest. On this occasion, however, you will also be rewarded with a view of a pristine beach where rainforest meets the Coral Sea. To the north over 200 kilometres away, lies Cooktown.

Cape Tribulation, incidentally, was named by Captain James Cook afte the "Endeavour" hit a reef offshore - and limped to what is now Cooktown.

Cape Tribulation was named by James Cook after his ship struck a reef off-shore and was badly damaged.

Cooktown, the site where James Cook beached the "Endeavour" in 1770.

Cooktown

On 10th June, 1770, Captain James Cook hit a reef aboard the "Endeavour" whilst exploring the far north of Australia's coastline. Unlike many other ships, the "Endeavour" survived the experience, limped north and entered the mouth of a river which now bears the ship's name.

The site where Captain Cook beached the ship on 17th June, 1770, is now called Cooktown. Fortunately, the local aboriginals - the Guugu Yimidhirr tribe - proved friendly and hospitable, and Captain Cook and his crew stayed a total of 48 days, repairing the vessel and resting before sailing back to England.

After James Cook departed, history virtually stood still for one hundred years. Then, on 3rd September, 1873, it was reported that James Venture Mulligan had discovered large quantities of gold at Palmer River.

"Gold fever" quickly brought prospectors and Cook's Town, now Cooktown, was officially born on 25th October, 1873. Within a very short time, the town had a booming, brawling population that reached 33,000 people (including 20,000 Chinese). The town boasted over 60 pubs, and was soon Queensland's second largest settlement.

However, as the goldfields waned, so did Cooktown. A major cyclone in 1907 contributed to its demise - destroying or damaging all of the ships in the harbour and flattening many of the town's buildings.

Today, the complete shire of Cooktown, which is almost the size of

Local inhabitants renact Captain's Cook Landing each year.

The Westpac Bank still has its original cedar furnishings.

In the gold-rush days Cooktown had over 60 Hotels.

England, has just 5,000 inhabitants – and Cooktown itself still has all the atmosphere of a remote, frontier town. This is hardly surprising since land access to Cooktown is restricted to a rugged inland road (340 kms) or coastal road (235 kms), both suitable only for four wheel drive vehicles.

Despite its isolated location, a surprising number of visitors find their way to Cooktown and few are disappointed by the experience. Although the trip by road is an adventure many look forward to, travellers can now cruise to Cooktown by high-powered catamaran from Port Douglas in just two and a half hours, or fly up from Cairns in around 35 minutes.

Each year in June, on the Queen's Birthday, the landing of Cook is re-enacted in June – and this colourful event attracts all the colourful locals!

The James Cook Historical Museum should be visited as it has many interesting items on display, including the original anchor from the "Endeavour", and relics of the Palmer River gold rush.

Even the Cooktown cemetery is interesting. There is a Chinese Shrine, a memorial to the many Chinese who joined the gold rush in the late 1800's and then died here. You will also find the grave of Mary Watson, the famous "heroine of Lizard Island".

Visitors should also head up to the quaint, corrugated iron light-house on the top of Grassy Hill. Captain Cook climbed this high hill in 1770 to chart his passage north – and visitors today can enjoy panoramic views across the reef, hinterland and township.

Other attractions in the area include the mysterious Black Mountain and Lion's Den, surely one of the world's most isolated pubs. Be sure to look at the old piano in the saloon – on top there are several large glass containers of pickled snakes which eye the close observer!

The Lion's Den Hotel, a pub full of character, is 35 kilometres south of Cooktown. It was built in 1875.

The Islands

Beautiful Lizard Island lies about 270 kilometres north of Cairns.

Within the Great Barrier Reef region there are about 900 islands. Most are small, uninhabited and rarely visited except by yachtsmen because of their isolated locations but some of great beauty can be easily reached from Cairns and Port Douglas. Three islands - Lizard, Green and Fitzroy - have resorts where holiday-makers can enjoy a temporary sanctuary from the pressures of our modern world.

Many of the islands have long been important sanctuaries for wild-life. In fact, the islands within the Great Barrier Reef region are inhabited or visited by over 240 species of birds. Some islands attract noisy colonies of tens of thousands of birds. Other islands provide secluded nesting sites for turtles.

There are two different types of islands within the Great Barrier Reef region - coral cays and continental islands.

Continental islands were once mountain peaks on the coastline of Australia. When sea levels rose after the last Ice Age, islands were formed and extensive coral reefs have developed around many of them.

Cays are much smaller and lower than continental islands - most are not much more than four metres above sea level. Coral cays are islands that have actually developed on reefs over thousands of years. Cays are created as coral debris accumulates at the sheltered side of the reef that it sits on. Slowly a sand-bank forms and vegetation takes hold as birds leave droppings with seeds. Other seeds are washed or blown ashore.

Perhaps one of the most enjoyable and recommended day-trips is to Michaelmas Cay, about 40 kilometres north-west of Cairns. This small, uninhabited island has a superb beach all around it, and warm crystal-clear water, perfect for swimming and snorkelling. It is also a haven to thousands of Noddy Terns in the nesting season.

Pleasure cruises have gone to Green Island since 1890.

A popular way to explore the Reef and its Islands is aboard this luxurious cruise ship, the "Reef Endeavour", which cruises regularly from Cairns to Cooktown.

Green Island is a larger coral cay 27 kilometres off Cairns which is covered by far denser vegetation. Over 40 species of shrubs and trees can be found on this island including enormous Fig trees, Grey Boxwood and Northern Yellow Boxwood trees, Beach Almonds and Drooping Sheoaks. Boats cruise out to the island daily where there is an underwater Observatory which allows you to see many examples of the Reef's marine-life. The island has a small resort for those who wish to stay longer than just a day.

Fitzroy Island is a continental island 24 kilometres east of Cairns. It, too, has a small resort (and camping grounds), and can also be visited for just one day. Fitzroy has areas of lush rainforest where some of Australia's largest and most colourful butterflies can be found. Some of the trees are extremely old. One particular specimen, a Zamia Palm, is estimated to be nearly 1,000 years old.

A boat also cruises daily to Normanby Island, which is part of the Franklin Islands, a group of small, uninhabited, picturesque islands south of Cairns. They offer very beautiful, unspoiled beaches and excellent fringing reefs. The boat leaves from Deeral, on the Mulgrave River, about one hour south of Cairns (a coach connection is available).

Low Island can be reached from Port Douglas. Boats cruise daily to this small, coral cay - vegetated with numerous exotic plants, and a site for a light-house since 1878 - for a day of relaxation, snorkelling and diving.

Lizard Island is 270 kilometres and about one hour's flight north of Cairns. It has a large, stunning lagoon with acres of coral, and a small exclusive resort. The island has 24 beaches, wonderful snorkelling and diving, and the waters around it are some of the world's best fishing grounds for Black Marlin. Harry Secombe, the English comedian, left this message in the guest book at the Lodge after his third visit: "If I ruled the world I'd rule it from Lizard Island."

The Low Isles is a wonderful day trip from Port Douglas. Quicksilver's "Wavedancer" catamaran, moored off-shore, sails here daily..

Michaelmas Cay is just 40 kilometres north-east of Cairns - but could be a million!

Michaelmas Cay, although small, is an important bird sanctuary - and a wonderful day excursion from Cairns.

The Great Barrier Reef is home to over 400 kinds of coral and 1,500 species of fish.

The Great Barrier Reef

The Great Barrier Reef is actually made up of almost 3,000 individual coral reefs - the largest single reef system in the world - and was declared a World Heritage Site in 1981.

The Great Barrier Reef covers a vast area of approximately 350,000 square kilometres. This makes it greater in size than either Victoria or the United Kingdom, and half the size of Texas. This huge patchwork of reefs begins in the Torres Strait, which separates New Guinea and Australia, and runs down the north-eastern coast of Australia for 2,500 kilometres.

Visitors to the Cairns area have ready access to several outer reefs, as well a number of islands which have their own fringing reefs.

Rich in Marine Life.

The Great Barrier Reef harbours an incredible array of marine life. There are over 400 kinds of colourful hard and soft corals to be found in the region and more than 1,500 species of fish.

The Great Barrier Reef is the breeding ground, too, for some of the world's endangered animal species. Each year, Humpback whales journey 5,000 kilometres to the Great Barrier Reef all the way from the Antarctic to mate and give birth to their calves.

The Reef is also one of the most important habitats for sea turtles. Of the planet's seven species of sea turtles, three breed on the Reef.

The islands within the Great Barrier Reef region are also inhabited or

Snorkellers explore the colourful underwater world of the Reef.

High-speed catamarans take people to the outer reefs. This is the Quicksilver pontoon at Agincourt Reef, east of Port Douglas.

visited by over 240 species of birds.

Since becoming a World Heritage Site, the Park has been under the protection of the Federally funded Great Barrier Marine Park Authority. Activities prohibited include oil exploration, mining, and the taking of certain specimens of fish or shell species. Rangers patrol the Marine Park aboard both aircraft and boats - and by using information gathered by scientists, and properly managing human activity in the Marine Park, the Authority aims to preserve the Reef and its rich resources for future generations.

Created by billions of coral polyps.

The Great Barrier Reef is the largest structure ever created on the earth by living organisms. The principal engineers of this vast labyrinth of reefs are organisms so small that they are barely visible to the human eye.

These tiny animals are called coral polyps and in hard corals, each polyp builds an external, cup-like skeleton of calcium carbonate. As a founder polyp constantly divides a coral colony is formed.

Different corals grow at different rates. Staghorn corals can grow as much as 20 to 30 centimetres a year. Other corals can grow as little as three millimetres in the same period.

Corals feed on microscopic animals floating in the water around them. They catch these minute animals by using tentacles which are armed with barbed darts of stinging cells (fortunately, the stinging darts of most corals have little effect on humans because our skin is too thick for them to penetrate).

The many beautiful colours of live corals are produced by pigments in the outer layers of coral tissue, and by the minute zooxanthellae plant cells and other algae found in their skeletons. Together, the pigments and algae can give corals brilliant colours such as red, green and yellow.

As hard corals die, they are cemented together by their own limestone. As this process is repeated, a reef many metres thick is gradually built up with living corals on its surface providing shelter and food for countless fish, starfish, molluscs and other animals.

Coral colonies come in many different sizes and shapes. These are reflected in names like Mushroom, Plate, Staghorn and Brain corals.

Visiting the Reef.

From Cairns, several companies operate high speed catamarans or luxury sailing boats out to the Reef and its islands (see previous chapter). At Moore, Norman and Arlington Reefs there are large, permanently moored pontoons where snorkellers and divers can explore the Reef's colourful underwater life. Excursions depart from Trinity Wharf. Out at the reefs, you can also view the underwater life in glass-bottom boats and semi-submersible craft.

From Port Douglas, you can go out to Agincourt Reef where there is also a pontoon for snorkellers and divers, and a semi-submersible craft for those who would prefer to keep their feet dry.

There are companies and vessels which also specialise exclusively in dive charters from both Cairns and Port Douglas for just one day or lengthier periods.

Other vessels offers three, four and seven days cruises for non-divers, taking passengers to the outer reefs and beautiful, uninhabited islands for beachcombing, swimming, snorkelling - and just sheer relaxation. Information about such charters and cruises can be obtained from the Queensland Government Travel Centre or the Far North Queensland Promotion Bureau.

Helicopters and sea-planes are also available for flights from Cairns and they give a spectacular bird's-eye view of the Reef. These flights are highly recommended by the author.

Many islands are important nesting sites for birds.

A Noddy Tern protects its egg from the sun's harsh heat.

A diver, surrounded by colourful soft corals, hard corals and sponges, observes a small school of violet Anthiases or Fairy Basslets.

Anemone fish are immune to the stinging tentacles of an anemone and hide among them when threatened by predators.

A Golden Damsel fish grows to a length of about 12 centimetres.

A Chromodoris Elizabethina Nudibranch. These creatures feed on sponges.

A Barramundi Cod shelters under a Plate Coral.

The fiercesome looking Ragged-Finned Firefish eats smaller fish.

A small Spider Crab sits on a Gorgonian Coral. The tiny white "flowers" scattered over the coral are its polyps.

The beautiful Blue Spotted Coral Cod can grow up to 30 centimetres in length.

A Whip Goby rests on a Gorgonian Coral. This tiny fish feeds on plankton.

Parrot fish start life as females and then some turn into males.

A brightly coloured yellow and black Flatworm glides by a Daisy Coral.

Clown Anemone fish have a very striking colour pattern.

A large school of Diagonal Banded Sweetip.

A Blue Spotted Coral Cod floats through a underwater garden of soft corals, sponges, and Gorgonian corals.

Directory – Useful Names and Addresses

Below are a number of addresses and phone numbers you may find useful during your stay, or whilst planning your visit to Far North Queensland. More detailed information on hotels, motels, holiday units and back-packer accommodation - and the area's many tour and excursion operators - can be obtained through the Queensland Government Travel Centre, Accommodation Services or Information Centres listed below.

TOURIST INFORMATION CENTRES

Queensland Govt Travel Centre
243 Edward Street,
Brisbane, Qld. 4000
Tel: (07) 3874 2800
Fax: (07) 3221 5320
Information and travel/accommodation booking service, cruises.

Tourism Tropical North Queensland Information Centre
The Cairns Esplanade,
Cairns, Qld. 4870.
Tel: (07) 4051 3588
Fax: (07) 4051 0127

Queensland Parks & Wildlife Service
10-12 McLeod Street,
Cairns, Qld. 4870.
Tel: (07) 4052 3095
Guides, maps, camping permits for National Parks.

CRUISE SHIPS

Captain Cook Cruises
Trinity Wharf,
Cairns, 4870.
Tel: (07) 4031 4433
Toll free 1800 221 080
www.captaincook.com.au
Offers 3, 4 & 7-night Reef cruises aboard "Reef Endeavour", visiting Cooktown, uninhabited coral cays, outer reefs and islands including Lizard & Dunk.

DAY EXCURSIONS/ FISHING

Cairns Reef Charter Services
Marlin Parade,
Cairns, Qld. 4870.
Tel: (07) 4031 4742
Fax: (07) 4031 4610
Specialising in game-fishing charters.

Cairns Game Fishing Club
Marlin Parade,
Cairns, Qld. 4870
Tel: (07) 4051 5979

Great Adventures
Wharf Street, Cairns, 4870.
Tel: (07) 4051 5644
Tour company operating boats to Green Island, Fitzroy Island, and Norman and Moore Reefs.

Kuranda Scenic Railway
QR Travel Centre,
Bunda St., Cairns, 4870
Tel: (07) 4036 9249

Ocean Spirit Cruises
33 Lake Street,
Cairns, 4870
Tel: (07) 4031 2920
Luxury sailing catamarans

visiting Michaelmas & Upolu Cays daily.

Quicksilver Connections
Marina Mirage,
Port Douglas, Qld. 4871.
Tel: (07) 4099 5455
Port Douglas tour company operating boats to Agincourt Reef & the Low Isles.

Skyrail Rainforest Cableway
Cnr. Kamerunga Rd. & Cook Highway,
Smithfield, Cairns, Q 4878.
Tel: (07) 4038 1555
Scenic Rainforest Cableway to Kuranda.

Sunlover Cruises
Trinity Wharf,
Cairns, 4870
Tel: (07) 4050 1333
Cruises to Fitzroy Is, Moore & Arlington Reefs.

Tjapukai Aboriginal Cultural Park
Cnr. Kamerunga Rd. & Cook Highway,
Smithfield, Qld. 4878
Tel: (07) 4042 9999

ACCOMMODATION SERVICES

Accom Cairns
25 Sheridan Street,
Cairns, Qld. 4870
Tel: (07) 4051 3200
Fax: (07) 4031 1813
Accommodation booking service for holiday apartments in Cairns, the Northern beaches and Port Douglas.

HOTELS/RESORTS

Lizard Island Lodge
PMB 40, Cairns, 4870

Tel: (07) 4060 3999
Fax: (07) 4060 3991
Toll-free reservations:
132 469

Radisson Plaza Hotel
Pierpoint Road,
Cairns, 4870
Tel: (07) 4031 1411

Sheraton-Mirage Port Douglas
Davidson Street,
Port Douglas, 4871
Tel: (07) 4099 5888

Silky Oaks Lodge
Finlay Vale Road,
Mossman, 4873
Tel: (07) 4098 1666
Toll-free reservations:
132 469
Lodge overlooking Daintree River.

Sovereign Resort
Charlotte Street,
Cooktown, 4871
Tel: (07) 4069 5400

AIRLINES

Aquaflight Airways
Shop J3, The Pier,
Cairns, 4870.
Tel: (07) 4031 4307
Scenic seaplane flights to Green Island and Reef.

Heli Adventures
Cairns Airport
Tel: (07) 4034 9066
Scenic helicopter excursions to the Reef and Rainforest.

Trans State
Cairns Airport
Tel: (07) 4035 9722
Operates daily flights between Cairns & Cooktown.

DIVING

Cairns Dive Centre
1/135 Abbott Street,
Cairns, 4870
Tel: (07) 4051 0294
Diver training facility & dive trips to the Reef.

Mike Ball Dive Expeditions
28 Spence Street,
Cairns, 4870
Tel: (07) 4031 5484
Liveaboard dive vessels.

Pro Dive Cairns
116 Spence Street,
Cairns, 4870
Tel: (07) 4031 5255
Dive courses, liveaboard trips.

A WARM CLIMATE ALL YEAR ROUND

	Max Temp Deg. C	Min Temp Deg. C	Daily hours of Sunshine
January	32	24	7.1
February	31	23	6.4
March	30	22	6.6
April	29	21	6.2
May	29	19	6.5
June	26	17	6.0
July	25	16	6.9
August	26	16	7.4
September	28	17	7.7
October	29	20	8.4
November	31	21	8.5
December	32	23	7.7

NOTE: The Tropical Far North has two pronounced seasons - The Wet Season and the Dry Season. Rainfall and humidity can be high in January, February and March during the Wet Season, and unsealed roads in the wilderness areas north of the Daintree River can be difficult to travel on, or even impassable, for even 4-wheel drive vehicles. May through to December are the best months to visit - with August, September, October and November usually being near perfect.

Acknowledgements

The photographs in this book were taken by David Heenan with the exception of those listed below. The author would like to thank the individuals and organisations who provided these extra images. He would especially like to acknowledge Lincoln Fowler who provided many of the additional photographs.

Captain Cook Cruises: Plate 1, pg 80.
John Oxley Library: Historical images, pages 8-17, except plate 1, pg.11; plate 2, pg.30.
Lincoln Fowler: Plate 1, pg.1; plate 1, pg.5; plate 1, pg.18; plate 1, pg.22; plate 1, pg.23; plate 1, pg.34; plate 1, pg.39; plate 1, pg. 41; plate 2, pg.46; plate 1, pg.62; plate 1, pg.69; plate 1, pg.72; plate 1, pg.74; plate 1, pg.75; plates 1&2, pg. 76; plate 1, pg.77; plate 1, pg.78.
Paradise Palms Golf Course: Plate 1, pg.25.
Port Douglas Picture Library: Plates 1& 4, pg.37; plate 3, pg.49; plate 1, pg.53; plate 1, pg. 54; plate 1, pg.61; plate 1, pg.71; plate 1, pg. 82; plate 1, pg.85; plate 1, pg. 93.
Queensland Department of Environment & Heritage: plate 1, pg.40; plate 1, pg.44; plate 1, pg.66; plates 1&2, pg.70; plate 1, pg.73.
Queensland Tourist & Travel Corporation: Plate 2, pg.22; plate 2, pg.23; plate 2, pg.27; plate 1, pg.42; plate 2, pg.49; plate 1, pg.53; plate 1, pg.64.
Quicksilver Connections: Plate 1, pg. 86.
Nick Tonks: Underwater images: Pages 88-92, 94-5.
Tjapukai Aboriginal Cultural Park: Plate 1, pg.33
Shawn Wallace: Plate 2, pgs. 2&3